The Defence of
Duffer's Drift

by

Ernest Dunlop Swinton

Table of Contents

The United States Infantry Association Officers

President. Major-General J.C. BATES, U.S. Army.

Vice-President. Lieutenant-Colonel JAS. S. PETTIT, U.S. Infantry. Assistant Adjutant-General.

Secretary and Treasurer. Captain BENJAMIN ALVORD, General Staff.

Executive Council. Lieutenant-Colonel JAMES S. PETTIT, U.S. Infantry

A.A.G. Major WM. P. EVANS, U.S. Infantry

A.A.G. Major JOHN S. MALLORY, 12th Infantry

G.S. Captain BENJAMIN ALVORD, 25th Infantry

G.S. Captain H.C. HALE, 15th Infantry, G.S. Captain

C.H. MUIR, 2d Infantry

G.S. Captain FRANK MCINTYRE, 19th Infantry

G.S. Captain D.E. NOLAN, 30th Infantry, G.S.

Prologue

Upon an evening after a long and tiring trek, I arrived at Dreamdorp. The local atmosphere, combined with a heavy meal, are responsible for the following nightmare, consisting of a series of dreams. To make the sequence of the whole intelligible, it is necessary to explain that, though the scene of each vision was the same, yet by some curious mental process I had no recollection of the place whatsoever. In each dream the locality was totally new to me, and I had an entirely fresh detachment. Thus I had not the great advantage of working over familiar ground. One thing, and one only, was carried on from dream to dream, and that was the vivid recollection of the general lessons previously learnt. These finally produced success.

The whole series of dreams, however, remained in my memory as a connected whole when I awoke.

First Dream

"Any fool can get into a hole."—Old Chinese proverb.

"If left to you, for defence make spades."—Bridge Maxim.

I felt lonely, and not a little sad, as I stood on the bank of the river near Duffer's Drift and watched the red dust haze, raised by the southward departing column in the distance, turn slowly into gold as it hung in the afternoon sunlight. It was just three o'clock, and here I was on the banks of the Silliaasvogel river, left behind by my column with a party of fifty N.C.O.'s and men to hold the drift. It was an important ford, because it was the only one across which wheeled traffic could pass for some miles up or down the river.

The river was a sluggish stream, not now in flood, crawling along at the very bottom of its bed between steep banks which were almost vertical, or at any rate too steep for wagons everywhere except at the drift itself. The banks from the river edge to their tops and some distance outwards were covered with dense thorn and other bushes, which formed a screen impenetrable to the sight. They were also broken by small ravines and holes, where the earth had been eaten away by the river when in flood, and were consequently very rough.

Some two thousand odd yards north of the drift was a flat-topped, rocky mountain, and about a mile to the northeast appeared the usual sugar-loaf kopje, covered with bushes and boulders—steep on the south, but gently falling to the north; this had a farm on the near side of it. About a thousand yards

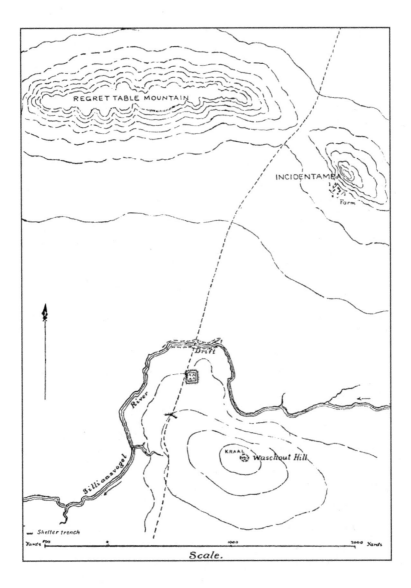

south of the drift was a convex and smooth hill, somewhat like an inverted basin, sparsely sown with small boulders, and with a Kaffir kraal, consisting of a few grass and mud huts on top. Between the river and the hills on the north the ground consisted of open and almost level veldt; on the south bank the veldt was more undulating, and equally open. The whole place was covered with ant-hills.

My orders were—to hold Duffer's Drift at all costs. That I should probably be visited by some column within three or four days' time. That I might possibly be attacked before that time, but that this was very unlikely, as no enemy were known to be within a hundred miles. That the enemy had guns.

It all seemed plain enough except that the true inwardness of the last piece of information did not strike me at the time. Though in company with fifty "good men and true," it certainly made me feel somewhat lonely and marooned to be left out there comparatively alone on the boundless veldt; but the chance of an attack filled me, and, I am quite sure, my men with martial ardor; and at last here was the chance I had so often longed for. This was my first "show," my first independent command, and I was determined to carry out my orders to the bitter end. I was young and inexperienced, it is true, but I had passed all my examinations with fair success; my men were a good willing lot, with the traditions of a glorious regiment to uphold, and would, I knew, do all I should require of them. We were also well supplied with ammunition and rations; and had a number of picks, shovels and sandbags, etc., which I confess had been rather forced on me.

As I turned towards my gallant little detachment, visions of a bloody and desperate fight crossed my mind—a fight to the last cartridge, and then an appeal to cold steel, with ultimate victory—and—— But a discreet cough at my elbow brought me back to realities, and warned me that my color-sergeant was waiting for orders.

After a moment's consideration, I decided to pitch my small camp on a spot just south of the drift, because it was slightly rising ground, which I knew should be chosen for a camp whenever possible. It was, moreover, quite close to the drift, which was also in its favor, for, as everyone knows, if you are told off to guard anything, you mount a guard quite close to it, and place a sentry, if possible, standing on top of it. The place picked out by me also had the river circling round three sides of it in a regular horseshoe bend, which formed a kind of ditch, or, as the book says, "a natural obstacle." I was indeed lucky to have such an ideal place close at hand; nothing could have been more suitable.

I came to the conclusion that, as the enemy were not within a hundred miles, there would be no need to place the camp in a state of defence till the following day. Besides, the men were tired after their long trek, and it would be quite as much as they could do comfortably to arrange nice and shipshape all the stores and tools, which had been dumped down anyhow in a heap, pitch the camp, and get their teas before dark.

Between you and me, I was really relieved to be able to put off my defensive measures till the morrow, because I was a wee bit puzzled as to what to do. In fact, the more I thought, the more puzzled I grew. The only "measures of defence" I could recall for the moment were, how to tie "a thumb or overhand knot," and how long it takes to cut down an apple tree of six inches' diameter. Unluckily neither of these useful facts seemed quite to apply. Now, if they had given me a job like fighting the battle of Waterloo, or Sedan, or Bull Run, I knew all about that, as I had crammed it up and been examined in it, too. I also knew how to take up a position for a division, or even an army corps, but the stupid little subaltern's game of the defence of a drift with a small detachment was, curiously enough, most perplexing. I had never really considered such a thing. However, in the light of my habitual dealings with army corps, it would, no doubt, be child's-play after a little thought.

Having issued my immediate orders accordingly, I decided to explore the neighborhood, but was for a moment puzzled as to which direction I should take; for, having no horse, I could not possibly get all round before dark. After a little thought, it flashed across my mind that obviously I should go to the north. The bulk of the enemy being away to the north, that, of course, must be the front. I knew naturally that there must be a front, because in all the schemes I had had to prepare, or the exams I had undergone, there was always a front, or—"the place where the enemies come from." How often, also, had I not had trouble in getting out of a dull sentry which his "front" and what his "beat" was. The north, then, being my front, the east and west were my flanks, where there might possibly be enemies, and the south was my rear, where naturally there were none.

I settled these knotty points to my satisfaction, and off I trudged, with my field-glasses and, of course, my kodak, directing my steps towards the Dutch farm, with gleaming white walls, nestling under the kopje to the northeast. It was quite a snug little farm for South Africa, surrounded by blue gums and fruit trees. About a quarter of a mile from the farm I was met by the owner, Mr. Andreas Brink, a tame or surrendered Boer farmer, and his two sons, Piet and Gert. Such a nice man, too, with a pleasant face and long beard. He would insist on calling me "captain," and as any correction might have confused him, I did not think it worth while to make any, and after all I wasn't so very far from my "company." The three of them positively bristled with dog's-eared and dirty passes from every provost marshal in South Africa, which they insisted on showing me. I had not thought of asking for them, and was much impressed; to have so many they must be special men. They escorted me to the farm, where the guid wife and several daughters met us, and gave me a drink of milk, which was most acceptable after my long and dusty trek. The whole family appeared either to speak or to understand English, and we had a very friendly chat, during the course of which I gathered that there were no Boer commandoes anywhere within miles; that the whole family cordially hoped that there never would be again, and that Brink was really a most loyal Briton, and had been much against the war, but had been forced to go on commando with his two sons. Their loyalty was evident, because there was an oleograph of the Queen on the wall, and one of the numerous flappers was playing our National anthem on the harmonium as I entered.

The farmer and the boys took a great interest in all my personal gear, especially a brand-new pair of latest-pattern field-glasses, which they tried with much delight, and many exclamations of "Allermachtig." They evidently appreciated them extremely, but could not imagine any use for my kodak in war-time, even after I had taken a family group. Funny, simple fellows! They asked and got permission from me to sell milk, eggs, and butter in the camp, and I strolled on my way congratulating myself on the good turn I was thus able to do myself and detachment, none of whom had even smelt such luxuries for weeks.

After an uneventful round, I directed my steps back towards the thin blue threads of smoke, rising vertically in the still air, which alone showed the position of my little post, and as I walked the peacefulness of the whole scene impressed me. The landscape lay bathed in the warm light of the setting sun, whose parting rays tinged most strongly the various heights within view, and the hush of approaching evening was only broken by the distant lowing of oxen, and by the indistinct and cheerful hum of the camp, which gradually grew louder as I approached. I strolled along in quite a pleasant frame of mind, meditating over the rather curious names which Mr. Brink had given me for the surrounding features of the landscape. The kopje above his farm was called Incidentamba, the flat-topped mountain some two miles to the north was called Regret Table Mountain, and the gently rising hill close to the drift on the south of the river was called Waschout Hill. Everything was going on well, and the men were at their teas when I got back. The nice Dutchman, with his apostolic face, and the lanky Piet and Gert, were already there, surrounded by a swarm of men, to whom they were selling their wares at exorbitant rates. The three of them strolled about the camp, showing great interest in everything, asking most intelligent questions about the British forces and the general position of affairs, and seemed really relieved to have a strong British post near. They did not even take offence when some of the rougher men called them "blarsted Dutchmen," and refused to converse with them, or buy their "skoff." About dusk they left, with many promises to return with a fresh supply on the morrow.

After writing out my orders for next day—one of which was for digging some trenches round the camp, an operation which I knew my men, as becomes good British soldiers, disliked very much, and regarded as fatigues—I saw the two guards mounted, one at the drift, and the other some little way down the river, each furnishing one sentry on the river bank.

When all had turned in, and the camp was quite silent, it was almost comforting to hear the half-hourly cry of the sentries—"Number one—all is well;" "Number two—all is well." By this sound I was able to locate them, and knew they were at their proper posts. On going round sentries about midnight, I was pleased to find that they were both alert, and that, as it was a cold night, each guard had built a bonfire, silhouetted in the cheerful blaze of which stood the sentry—a clear-cut monument to all round that here was a British sentry fully on the qui-vive. After impressing them with their orders, the extent of their "beat," and the direction of their "front," etc., I turned in. The fires they had built, besides being a comfort to themselves, were also useful to me, because twice during the night when I looked out I could, without leaving my tent, plainly see them at their posts. I finally fell asleep, and dreamt of being decorated with a crossbelt made of V.C.'s and D.S.O.'s and of wearing red tabs all down my back.

*   *   *   *   *

I was suddenly awoken, about the grey of dawn, by a hoarse cry—"Halt! who goes——" cut short by the unmistakable "plip-plop" of a Mauser rifle. Before I was off my valise, the reports of Mausers rang around the camp from every side; these, mingled with the smack of the bullets as they hit the ground and stripped the "zipzip" of the leaden hail through the tents, and the curses and groans of men who were hit as they lay or stumbled about trying to get out, made a hellish din. There was some wild shooting in return from my men, but it was all over in a moment, and as I managed to wriggle out of my tent the whole place was swarming with bearded men, shooting into the heaving canvas. At that moment I must have been clubbed on the head, for I knew no more until I found myself seated on an empty case having my head, which was dripping with blood, tied up by one of my men.

$$*\quad*\quad*\quad*\quad*$$

Our losses were ten men killed, including both sentries, and twenty-one wounded; the Boers, one killed and two wounded.

$$*\quad*\quad*\quad*\quad*$$

Later on, as, at the order of the not ill-natured but very frowzy Boer commandant, I was gloomily taking off the saucy warm spotted waistcoat knitted for me by my sister, I noticed our friends of the previous evening in very animated and friendly conversation with the burghers, and "Pappa" was, curiously enough, carrying a rifle and bandolier and my new field-glasses. He was laughing and pointing towards something lying on the ground, through which he finally put his foot. This, to my horror, I recognized as my unhappy camera. Here, I suppose, my mind must have slightly wandered, for I found myself repeating some Latin lines, once my favorite imposition, but forgotten since my school-days—

"Timeo Danaos et dona ferentes——"

when suddenly the voice of the field cornet broke into my musing with "Your breeches, too, captain."

*   *   *   *   *

Trekking all that day on foot, sockless, and in the boots of another, I had much to think of besides my throbbing head. The sight of the long Boer convoy with guns, which had succeeded so easily in crossing the drift I was to have held, was a continual reminder of my failure, and of my responsibility for the dreadful losses to my poor detachment. I gradually gathered from the Boers what I had already partially guessed, namely, that they had been fetched and guided all round our camp by friend Brink, had surrounded it in the dark, crawling about in the bush on the river bank, and had carefully marked down our two poor sentries. These they had at once shot on the alarm being given, and had then rushed the camp from the dense cover on three sides. Towards evening my head got worse, and its rhythmic throbbing seemed gradually to take a meaning, and hammered out the following lessons, the result of much pondering on my failure:

1. Do not put off taking your measures of defence till the morrow, as this is more important than the comfort of your men or the shipshape arrangement of your camp. Choose the position of your camp mainly with reference to your defence.

2. Do not in war-time show stray men of the enemy's breed all over your camp, be they never so kind and full of butter, and do not be hypnotized, by numerous "passes," at once to confide in them.

3. Do not let your sentries advertise their position to the whole world, including the enemy, by standing in the full glare of a fire, and making much noise every half hour.

4. Do not, if avoidable, be in tents when bullets are ripping through them: at such times a hole in the ground is worth many tents.

After these lessons had been dinned into my soul millions and millions of times, so that I could never forget them, a strange thing came to pass—there was a kaleidoscopic change, I had another dream.

Second Dream

"And what did ye look they should compass? Warcraft learnt in a breath, Knowledge unto occasion at the first far view of Death?"—KIPLING.

I suddenly found myself dumped down at Duffer's Drift with the same orders as already detailed, and an equal detachment composed of entirely different men. As before, and on every subsequent occasion, I had ample stores, ammunition, and tools. My position was precisely similar to my former one, with this important exception, running through my brain were four lessons.

As soon as I received my orders, therefore, I began to make out my plan of operations without wasting any time over the landscape, the setting sun, or the departing column, which, having off-loaded all our stores, soon vanished. I was determined to carry out all the lessons I had learnt as well as I knew how.

To prevent any strangers, friendly or otherwise, from coming into my position and spying out the elaborate defences I was going to make, I sent out at once two examining posts of one N.C.O. and three men each, one to the top of Waschout Hill, and the other some 1,000 yards out on the veldt to the north of the drift. Their orders were to watch the surrounding country, and give the alarm in the event of the approach of any body of men whatever (Boers were, of course, improbable, but still just possible), and also to stop any individuals, friendly or not, from coming anywhere near camp, and to shoot at once on non-compliance with the order to halt. If the new-comers had any provisions to sell, these were to be sent in with a list by one of the guard, who would return with the money, but the strangers were not to be allowed nearer the camp on any account.

Having thus arranged a safeguard against spies, I proceeded to choose a camping-ground. I chose the site already described in my former dream, and for the same reasons, which still appealed to me. So long as I was entrenched, it appeared the best place around. We started making our trenches as soon as I had marked off a nice squarish little enclosure which would about contain our small camp. Though, of course, the north was the front, I thought, having a camp, it would be best to have an all-round defence as a sort of obstacle. The majority of the men were told off to dig, which they did not relish, a few being detailed to pitch camp and prepare tea. As the length of trench was rather great for the available number of diggers, and the soil was hard, we were only able by dark, by which time the men were quite done up by their hard day, to make quite a low parapet and shallow trench. Still, we were "entrenched," which was the great thing, and the trench was all round our camp, so we were well prepared, even should we be attacked during the night or early next morning, which was out of the question.

During this time one or two strangers had approached the guard of the north from a farm under Incidentamba. As they had eggs and butter, etc., to sell, these were brought in as arranged for. The man sent in with the stuff reported that the elder of the Dutchmen was a most pleasant man, and had sent me a present of a pat of butter and some eggs, with his compliments, and would I allow him to come in and speak to me. However, not being such a fool as to allow him in my defences, I went out instead, in case he had any information. His only information was that there were no Boers anywhere near. He was an old man, but though he had a museum of "passes," I was not to be chloroformed by them into confidence. As he seemed friendly, and possibly loyal, I walked part of the way back to his farm with him, in order to look around. At dark the two examining posts came in, and two guards were mounted close by the object I was to watch, namely, the drift, at the same places as in my previous dream. This time, however, there was no half-hourly shouting, nor were there any fires, and the sentries had orders not to challenge but to shoot any person they might see outside camp at once. They were placed standing down the river bank, just high enough to see over the top, and were thus not unnecessarily exposed. Teas had been eaten, and all fires put out at dusk, and after dark all turned in, but in the trenches instead of in tents. After going round sentries to see everything snug for the night, I lay down myself with a sense of having done my duty, and neglected no possible precaution for our safety.

*   *   *   *   *

Just before dawn much the same happened as already described in my first dream, except that the ball was started by a shot without challenge from one of our sentries at something moving among the bush, which resulted in close range fire opening onto us from all sides. This time we were not rushed, but a perfect hail of bullets whistled in from every direction—from in front of each trench, along each trench, and from behind each trench, and over and through our parapet. It was sufficient to put a hand or head up to have a dozen bullets through and all round it, and the strange part was, we saw no one. As the detachment wag plaintively remarked, we could have seen lots of Boers, "if wasn't for the bushes in between."

After vainly trying until bright daylight to see the enemy in order to do some damage in return, so many men were hit, and the position seemed so utterly hopeless, that I had to hoist the white flag. We had by then twenty-four men killed and six wounded. As soon as the white flag went up the Boers ceased firing at once, and stood up; every bush and ant-hill up to 100 yards' range seemed to have hid a Boer behind it. This close range explained the marvelous accuracy of their shooting, and the great proportion of our killed (who were nearly all shot through the head) to our wounded.

As we were collecting ourselves preparatory to marching off, there were one or two things which struck me; one was that the Dutchman who had presented me with eggs and butter was in earnest confabulation with the Boer commandant, who was calling him "Oom" most affectionately. I also noticed that all the male Kaffirs from the neighboring kraal had been fetched and impressed to assist in getting the Boer guns and wagons across the drift and to load up our captured gear, and generally do odd and dirty jobs. These same Kaffirs did their work with amazing alacrity, and looked as if they enjoyed it; there was no "backchat" when an order was given—usually by friend "Oom."

Again, as I trudged with blistered feet that livelong day, did I think over my failure. It seemed so strange, I had done all I knew, and yet, here we were, ignominiously captured, twenty-four of us killed, and the Boers over the drift. "Ah, B.F., my boy," I thought, "there must be a few more lessons to be learnt besides those you already know," and in order to find out what these were, I pondered deeply over the details of the fight.

How the Boers must have known of our position, and how they had managed to get close up all round within snapshooting range without being discovered. What a tremendous advantage they had had in shooting from among the bushes on the bank, where they could not be seen, over us who had to show up over a parapet every time we looked for an enemy, and show up, moreover, just in the very place where every Boer expected us to, and was watching. There seemed to be some fault in the position. How the bullets seemed sometimes to come through the parapet, and how those that passed over one side hit the men defending the other side in the back. How on the whole that "natural obstacle," the river bed, seemed to be more of a disadvantage than a protection.

Eventually the following lessons framed themselves in my head—some of them quite new, some of them supplementing those four I had already learnt:

5. With modern rifles, to guard a drift or locality does not necessitate sitting on top of it (as if it could be picked up and carried away), unless the locality is suitable to hold for other and defensive reasons. It may even be much better to take up your defensive position some way from the spot, and so away from concealed ground, which enables the enemy to crawl up to very close range, concealed and unperceived, and to fire from cover which hides them even when shooting. It would be better, if possible, to have the enemy in the open, or to have what is called a clear "field of fire." A non-bullet proof parapet or shelter which is visible serves merely to attract bullets instead of keeping them out—the proof-thickness can be easily tested practically. When fired at by an enemy at close range from nearly all round, a low parapet and shallow trench are not of much use, as what bullets do not hit the defenders on one side hit those on another.

6. It is not enough to keep strange men of the enemy's breed away from your actual defences, letting them go free to warn their friends of your existence and whereabouts— even though they do not know the details of your defences. It would be very much better to gather in all such strangers and kindly, but firmly, to take care of them, so that they should not be under temptation to impart any knowledge they may have obtained. "Another way," as the cookery book says, more economical in lives, would be as follows: Gather and warmly greet a sufficiency of strangers. Stuff well with chestnuts as to the large force about to join you in a few hours; garnish with corroborative detail, and season according to taste with whiskey or tobacco. This will

very likely be sufficient for the nearest commando. Probable cost—some heavy and glib lying, but no lives will be expended.

7. It is not business to allow lazy black men (even though they be brothers and neutrals) to sit and pick their teeth outside their kraals whilst tired white men are breaking their hearts trying to do heavy labor in short time. It is more the duty of a Christian soldier to teach the dusky neutral the dignity of labor, and to keep him under guard, to prevent his going away to talk about it.

By the time the above lessons had been well burnt into my brain, beyond all chance of forgetfulness, a strange thing happened—I had a fresh dream.

Third Dream

"So when we take tea with a few guns, o' course you will know what to do—hoo! hoo!"—KIPLING.

I was at Duffer's Drift on a similar sunny afternoon and under precisely similar conditions, except that I now had seven lessons running through my mind.

I at once sent out two patrols, each of one N.C.O. and three men, one to the north and one to the south. They were to visit all neighboring farms and kraals and bring in all able-bodied Dutchmen and boys and male Kaffirs—by persuasion if possible, but by force if necessary. This would prevent the news of our arrival being carried around to any adjacent commandoes, and would also assist to solve the labor question. A small guard was mounted on the top of Waschout Hill as a look-out.

I decided that as the drift could not get up and run away, it was not necessary to take up my post or position quite close to it, especially as such a position would be under close rifle fire from the river bank, to which the approaches were quite concealed, and which gave excellent cover. The very worst place for such a position seemed to be anywhere within the horseshoe bend of the river, as this would allow an enemy practically to surround it. My choice, therefore, fell on a spot to which the ground gently rose from the river bank some 700 to 800 yards south of the drift. Here I arranged to dig a trench roughly facing the front (north) which thus would have about 800 yards clear ground on its front. We started to make a trench about fifty yards long for my fifty men, according to the usual rule.

Some little time after beginning, the patrols came in, having collected three Dutchmen and two boys, and about thirteen Kaffirs. The former, the leader of whom seemed a man of education and some importance, were at first inclined to protest when they were given tools to dig trenches for themselves, showed bundles of "passes," and talked very big about complaining to the General, and even as to a question in the "House" about our brutality. This momentarily staggered me, as I could not help wondering what might happen to poor B.F. if the member for Upper Tooting should raise the point; but Westminster was far away, and I hardened my heart. Finally they had the humor to see the force of the argument, that it was, after all, necessary, for their own health, as they would otherwise be out in the open veldt, should the post be attacked.

The Kaffirs served as a welcome relief to my men as they got tired. They also dug a separate hole for themselves on one side of and behind our trench, in a small ravine.

By evening we had quite a decent trench dug—the parapet was about two feet six inches thick at the top, and was quite bullet-proof, as I tested it. Our trench was not all in one straight line, but in two portions, broken back at a slight angle, so as to get a more divergent fire [rather cunning of me], though each half was of course as straight as I could get it.

It was astonishing what difficulty I had to get the men to dig in a nice straight line. I was particular as to this point, because I once heard a certain captain severely "told off" at manoeuvres by a very senior officer for having his trenches "out of dressing." No one could tell whether some "brass hat" might not come around and inspect us next day, so it was as well to be prepared for anything.

At dusk the guard on Waschout Hill, for whom a trench had also been dug, was relieved and increased to six men, and after teas and giving out the orders for the next day, we all "turned in" in our trenches. The tents were not pitched, as we were not going to occupy them, and it was no good merely showing up our position. A guard was mounted over our prisoners, or rather "guests," and furnished one sentry to watch over them.

Before falling asleep I ran over my seven lessons, and it seemed to me I had left nothing undone which could possibly help towards success. We were entrenched, had a good bullet-proof defence, all our rations and ammunition close at hand in the trenches, and water-bottles filled. It was with a contented feeling of having done everything right and of being quite "the little white-haired boy" that I gradually dozed off.

Next morning dawned brightly and uneventfully, and we had about an hour's work improving details of our trenches before breakfasts were ready. Just as breakfast was over, the sentry on Waschout Hill reported a cloud of dust away to the north, by Regret Table Mountain. This was caused by a large party of men mounted with wheeled transport of some sort. They were most probably the enemy, and seemed to be trekking in all innocence of our presence for the drift.

What a "scoop," I thought, if they come on quite unsuspecting, and cross the drift in a lump without discerning our position. I shall lie low, let the advanced party go past without a shot, and wait until the main body gets over this side within close range, and then open magazine fire into the thick of them. Yes, it will be just when they reach that broken ant-hill about 400 yards away that I shall give the word "Fire!"

However, it was not to be. After a short time the enemy halted, apparently for consideration. The advanced men seemed to have a consultation, and then gradually approached Incidentamba farm with much caution. Two or three women ran out and waved, whereupon these men galloped up to the farm at once. What passed, of course, we could not tell, but evidently the women gave information as to our arrival and position, because the effect was electrical. The advanced Boers split up into two main parties, one riding towards the river a long way to the east, and another going similarly to the west. One man galloped back with the information obtained to the main body, which became all bustle, and started off with their wagons behind Incidentamba, when they were lost to sight. Of course, they were all well out of range, and as we were quite ready, the only thing to do was to wait till they came out in the open within range, and then to shoot them down.

The minutes seemed to crawl—five, then ten minutes passed with no further sign of the enemy. Suddenly, "Beg pardon, sir; I think I see somethink on top of that kop-je on the fur side yonder." One of the men drew my attention to a few specks which looked like wagons moving about on the flatish shoulder of Incidentamba. Whilst I was focussing my glasses there was a "boom" from the hill, followed by a sharp report and a puff of smoke up in the air quite close by, then the sound as of heavy rain pattering down some two hundred feet in front of the trench, each drop raising its own little cloud of dust. This, of course, called forth the time-honored remarks of "What ho, she bumps!" and "Now we shan't be long," which proved only too true. I was aghast—I had quite forgotten the possibility of guns being used against me, though, had I remembered their existence, I do not know with my then knowledge, what difference it would have made to my defensive measures. As there was some little un-easiness among my men, I, quite cheerful in the security of our nice trench with the thick bullet-proof parapet, at once shouted out, "It's all right, men; keep under cover, and they can't touch us." A moment later there was a second boom, the shell whistled over our heads, and the hillside some way behind the trench was spattered with bullets.

By this time we were crouching as close as possible to the parapet, which, though it had seemed only quite a short time before so complete, now suddenly felt most woefully inadequate, with those beastly shells dropping their bullets down from the sky. Another boom. This time the shell burst well, and the whole ground in front of the trench was covered with bullets, one man being hit. At this moment rifle fire began on Waschout Hill, but no bullets came our way. Almost immediately another shot followed which showered bullets all over us; a few more men were hit, whose groans were unpleasant to listen to. Tools were seized, and men began frantically to try and dig themselves deeper into the hard earth, as our trench seemed to give no more protection from the dropping bullets than a saucer would from a storm of rain—but it was too late. We could not sink into the earth fast enough. The Boers had got the range of the trench to a nicety, and the shells burst over us now with a horrible methodic precision. Several men were hit, and there was no reason why the enemy should cease to rain shrapnel over us until we were all killed. As we were absolutely powerless to do anything, I put up the white flag. All I could do was to thank Providence that the enemy had no quick-firing field guns, or, though "we had not been long," we should have been blotted out before we could have hoisted it.

As soon as the gun-fire ceased, I was greatly surprised to find that no party of Boers came down from their artillery position on Incidentamba to take our surrender, but within three minutes some fifty Boers galloped up from the river bank on the east and the west, and a few more came up from the south round Waschout Hill. The guard on Waschout Hill, which had done a certain amount of damage to the enemy, had two men wounded by rifle fire. Not a single shell had come near them, though they were close to the Kaffir huts, which were plain enough.

*   *   *   *   *

What an anti-climax the reality had been from the pleasurable anticipations of the early morn, when I had first sighted the Boers.

Of course, the women on the farm had betrayed us, but it was difficult to make out why the Boers had at first halted and begun to be suspicious before they had seen the women at the farm. What could they have discovered? I failed entirely to solve this mystery.

During the day's trek the following lessons slowly evolved themselves, and were stored in my mind in addition to those already learnt:

8. When collecting the friendly stranger and his sons in order to prevent their taking information to the enemy of your existence and whereabouts, if you are wishful for a "surprise packet," do not forget also to gather his wife and his daughter, his manservant and his maidservant (who also have tongues), and his ox and his ass (which may possibly serve the enemy). Of course, if they are very numerous or very far off, this is impossible; only do not then hope to surprise the enemy.

9. Do not forget that, if guns are going to be used against you, a shallow trench with a low parapet some way from it is worse than useless, even though the parapet be bullet-proof ten times over. The trench gives the gunners an object to lay on, and gives no protection from shrapnel. Against well-aimed long-range artillery fire it would be better to scatter the defenders in the open, hidden in grass and bushes, or behind stones or ant-hills, than to keep them huddled in such a trench. With your men scattered around you can safely let the enemy fill your trench to the brim with shrapnel bullets.

10. Though to stop a shrapnel bullet much less actual thickness of earth is necessary than to stop a rifle bullet, yet this earth must be in the right place. For protection you must be able to get right close under the cover. As narrow a trench as possible, with the sides and inside of the parapet as steep as they will stand, will give you the best chance. To hollow out the bottom of the trench sides to give extra room will be even better, because the open top of the trench can be kept the less wide. The more like a mere slit the open

top of the trench is, the fewer shrapnel bullets will get in. While chewing over these lessons learnt from bitter experience, I had yet another dream.

Fourth Dream

"O wad some power the giftie gie us, To see oursels as others see us!"—BURNS.

Again did I find myself facing the same problem, this time with ten lessons to guide me. I started off by sending out patrols, as described in my last dream, but their orders were slightly different. All human beings were to be brought into our post, and any animals which could be of use to the enemy were to be shot, as we had no place for them.

For my defensive post I chose the position already described in my last dream, which seemed very suitable, for the reasons already given. We consequently dug a trench similar in plan to that already described, but, as I feared the possibility of guns being used against us, it was of a very different section. In plan it faced north generally, and was slightly broken forward to the front, each half being quite straight. In section it was about three feet six inches deep, with a parapet about twelve inches high in front of it; we made the trench as narrow as possible at the top compatible with free movement. Each man hollowed out the under part of the trench to suit himself, and made his own portion of the parapet to suit his height. The parapet was about two feet six inches thick at the top and quite steep inside, being built up of pieces of broken ant-heap, which were nearly as hard as stone.

The patrols returned shortly with their bag of a few men, women, and children. The women indulged in much useless abuse, and refused to obey orders, taking the matter less philosophically than their mankind. Here was evidently an opportunity of making use of the short training I had once had as A.D.C. I tried it. I treated the ladies with tons of "tact" in my suavest manner, and repeated the only Dutch words of comfort I knew—"Al zal recht kom"—but to no purpose. They had not been brought up to appreciate tact; in fact, they were not taking any. I turned regretfully round to the color-sergeant, winked solemnly and officially, and seeing an answering but respectful quiver in his left eyelid, said:

"Color-sergeant."

"Sir?"

"Which do you think is the best way of setting alight to a farm?"

"Well, sir, some prefer the large bedstead and straw, but I think the 'armonium and a little kerosene in one corner is as neat as anything."

There was no need for more—the ladies quite understood this sort of tact; the trouble was over.

The Dutchmen and Kaffirs were at once started digging shelters for themselves and the women and children. The latter were placed together, and were put into a small ravine not far from the trench, as it was necessary to place them in a really deep trench, firstly to keep them safe, and secondly to prevent their waving or signalling to the enemy. The existence of this ravine, therefore, saved much digging, as it only required some hollowing out at the bottom and a little excavation to suit admirably.

All dug with a will, and by night the shelters for the women and children and men prisoners, and the firing trench, were nearly done. All arrangements for the guards and sentries were the same as those described in the last dream, and after seeing everything was all correct and the ladies provided with tents to crawl under (they had their own blankets), I went to sleep with a feeling of well-earned security.

At daybreak next morning, as there were no signs of any enemy, we continued to improve our trench, altering the depth and alignment where necessary, each man suiting the size of the trench to his own legs. In the end the trench really looked quite neat, with the fresh red earth contrasting with the yellow of the veldt. As one of my reservists remarked, it only wanted an edging of oyster shells or ginger-beer bottles to be like his little "broccoli patch" at home. Upon these important details and breakfast a good two hours had been spent, when a force was reported to the north in the same position as described in the previous dream. It advanced in the same manner, except, of course, the advance men were met by no one at the farm. When I saw this, I could not help patting myself on the back and smiling at the Dutch ladies in the pit, who only scowled at me in return, and (whisper) spat!

The advanced party of the enemy came on, scouting carefully and stalking the farm as they came. As they appeared quite unwarned, I was wondering if I should be able to surprise them, all innocent of our presence, with a close-range volley, and then magazine fire into their midst, when suddenly one man stopped and the others gathered round him. This was when they were some 1,800 yards away, about on a level with the end of Incidentamba. They had evidently seen something and sniffed danger, for there was a short palaver and much pointing. A messenger then galloped back to the main body, which turned off behind Incidentamba with its wagons, etc. A small number, including a man on a white horse, rode off in a vague way to the west. The object of this move I could not quite see. They appeared to have a vehicle with them of some sort. The advanced party split up as already described. As all were still at long range, we could only wait.

Very shortly "boom" went a gun from the top of Incidentamba, and a shrapnel shell burst not far from us. A second and third followed, after which they soon picked up our range exactly, and the shell began to burst all about us; however, we were quite snug and happy in our nice deep trench, where we contentedly crouched. The waste of good and valuable shrapnel shell by the enemy was the cause of much amusement to the men, who were in great spirits, and, as one of them remarked, were "as cosy as cockroaches in a crack." At the expenditure of many shells two men only were hit—in the legs.

After a time the guns ceased fire, and we at once manned the parapet and stood up to repel an attack, but we could see no Boers, though the air began at once to whistle and hum with bullets. Nearly all these seemed to come from the river-bank in front, to the north and north-east, and kept the parapet one continual spirt of dust as they smacked into it. All we could do was to fire by sound at various likely bushes on the river-bank, and this we did with the greatest possible diligence, but no visible result.

In about a quarter of an hour we had had five men shot through the head, the most exposed part. The mere raising of a head to fire seemed to be absolutely fatal, as it had on a former occasion when we were attempting to fire at close range over a parapet against the enemy concealed. I saw two poor fellows trying to build up a pitiful little kind of house of cards with stones and pieces of anthill through which to fire. This was as conspicuous as a chimney-pot on top of the parapet, and was at once shot to powder before they had even used it, but not before it had suggested to me the remedy for this state of affairs. Of course, we wanted in such a case "head cover" and "loopholes." As usual, I was wise after the event, for we had no chance of making them then, even had we not been otherwise harassed. Suddenly the noise of firing became much more intense, but with the smack of the bullets striking the earth all round quite close it was not easy to tell from which direction this fresh firing came. At the same time the men seemed to be dropping much oftener, and I was impressing them with the necessity of keeping up a brisker fire to the front, when I noticed a bullet hit our side of the parapet.

It then became clear, the enemy must evidently have got into the donga behind us (to which I paid no attention, as it was to the rear), and were shooting us in the back as we stood up to our parapet.

This, I thought, must be what is called being "taken in reverse," and it was.

By the time I had gathered what was happening, about a dozen more men had been bowled over. I then ordered the whole lot to take cover in the trench, and only pop up to take a shot to the front or rear. But no more could be done by us towards the rear than to the front. The conditions were the same—no Boers to be seen. At this moment two of the guard from Waschout Hill started to run in to our trench, and a terrific fusillade was opened on to them, the bullets kicking up the dust all round them as they ran. One poor fellow was dropped, but the other managed to reach our trench and fall into it. He too was badly hit, but just had the strength to gasp out that except himself and the man who had started with him, all the guard on Waschout Hill had been killed or wounded, and that the Boers were gradually working their way up to the top. This was indeed cheering.

So hot was the fire now that no one could raise his head above ground without being shot, and by crouching down altogether and not attempting to aim, but merely firing our rifles over the edge of the trench, we remained for a short time without casualties. This respite, however, was short, for the men in the right half of the trench began to drop unaccountably whilst they were sitting well under cover, and not exposing themselves at all. I gradually discovered the cause of this. Some snipers must have reached the top of Waschout Hill, and were shooting straight down our right half trench. As the bullets snicked in thicker and thicker, it was plain the number of snipers was being increased.

This, I thought, must be being "enfiladed from a flank." It was so.

Without any order, we had all instinctively vacated the right half of our trench and crowded into the left half, which by great good luck could not be enfiladed from any point on the south side of the river, nor indeed by rifle-fire from anywhere, as, owing to the ground, its prolongation on the right was up above ground into the open air, and to the left did not touch ground for some 3,000 yards away on the veldt on the north bank.

Though we were huddled together quite helpless like rats in a trap, still it was in a small degree comforting to think that, short of charging the enemy could do nothing. For that we fixed bayonets and grimly waited. If they did make an assault, we had bayonets, and they had not, and we could sell our lives very dearly in a rough-and-tumble.

Alas! I was again deceived. There was to be no chance of close quarters and cold steel, for suddenly we heard, far away out on the veldt to the north, a sound as of some one beating a tin tray, and a covey of little shells whistled into the ground close by the trench; two of these burst on touching the ground. Right out of rifle-range, away on the open veldt on the north, I saw a party of Boers, with a white horse and a vehicle. Then I knew. But how had they managed to hit off so well the right spot to go to to enfilade our trench before they even knew where we were?

Pompom pompompom again, and the little steel devils ploughed their way into the middle of us in our shell-trap, mangling seven men. I at once diagnosed the position with great professional acumen—we were now enfiladed from both flanks, but the knowledge was acquired too late to help us, for—

"We lay bare as the paunch of the purser's sow,   To the hail of the Nordenfeldt."

This was the last straw; there was nothing left but surrender or entire annihilation at long range. I surrendered.

Boers, as usual, sprang up from all round. We had fought for three hours, and had twenty-five killed and seventeen wounded. Of these, seven only had been hit by the shrapnel and rifle-fire from the front. All the rest had been killed or hit from the flanks, where there should be few enemies, or the rear, where there should be none! This fact convinced me that my preconceived notions as to the front, and its danger relative to the other points of the compass, needed considerable modification. All my cherished ideas were being ruthlessly swept away, and I was plunged into a sea of doubt, groping for something certain or fixed to lay hold of. Could Longfellow, when he wrote that immortal line, "Things are not what they seem," ever have been in my position?

The survivors were naturally a little disheartened at their total discomfiture, when all had started so well with them in their "crack." This expressed itself in different ways. As one man said to a corporal, who was plugging a hole in his ear with a bit of rag—

"Somethink sickening, I call it, this enfilading racket; you never know which way it will take yer. I'm fairly fed up." To which the gloomy reply, "Enfiladed? Of course we've been enfiladed. This 'ere trench should have been wiggled about a bit, and then there would not have been quite so much of it. Yes, wiggled about—that's what it should have been." To which chipped in a third, "Yes, and somethink to keep the blighters from shooting us in the back wouldn't 'ave done us much 'arm, anyway."

There were evidently more things in earth than I had hitherto dreamt of in my philosophy!

*　　*　　*　　*　　*

As we trekked away to the north under a detached guard of Boers, many little points such as the above sank into my soul, but I could not for some time solve the mystery of why we had not succeeded in surprising the enemy. There were no men, women, children, or Kaffirs who knew of our arrival, who could have warned them. How did they spot our presence so soon, as they evidently must have done when they stopped and consulted in the morning? It was not until passing Incidentamba, as I casually happened to look round and survey the scene of the fight from the enemy's point of view, that I discovered the simple answer to the riddle. There on the smooth yellow slope of the veldt just south of the drift was a brownish-red streak, as plain as the Long Man of Wilmington on the dear old Sussex downs, which positively shrieked aloud, "Hi! hi! hi!—this way for the

British defence." I then grimly smiled to think of myself sitting like a "slick Alick" in that poster of a trench and expecting to surprise anybody!

Besides having been enfiladed and also taken in reverse, we had again found ourselves at a disadvantage as compared with the concealed enemy shooting at close range, from having to show up at a fixed place in order to fire.

Eventually I collected the following lessons:

11. For a small isolated post and an active enemy, there are no flanks, no rear, or, to put it otherwise, it is front all round.

12. Beware of being taken in reverse; take care, when placing and making your defences, that when you are engaged in shooting the enemy to the front of your trench, his pal cannot sneak up and shoot you in the back.

13. Beware of being enfiladed. It is nasty from one flank— far worse from both flanks. Remember, also, that though you may arrange matters so that you cannot be enfiladed by rifle-fire, yet you may be open to it from long range, by means of gun or pompom fire. There are few straight trenches that cannot be enfiladed from somewhere, if the enemy can only get there. You can sometimes prevent being enfiladed by so placing your trench that no one can get into prolongation of it to fire down it, or you can "wiggle" it about in many ways, so that it is not straight, or make "traverses" across it, or dig separate trenches for every two or three men.

14. Do not have your trench near rising ground over which you cannot see, and which you cannot hold.

15. Do not huddle all your men together in a small trench like sheep in a pen. Give them air.

16. As once before—cover from sight is often worth more than cover from bullets. For close shooting from a non-concealed trench, head cover with loopholes is an advantage. This should be bullet-proof and not be conspicuously on the top of the parapet, so as to draw fire, or it will be far more dangerous than having none.

17. To surprise the enemy is a great advantage.

18. If you wish to obtain this advantage, conceal your position. Though for promotion it may be sound to advertise your position, for defence it is not.

19. To test the concealment or otherwise of your position, look at it from the enemy's point of view.

Fifth Dream

"A trifling sum of misery New added to the foot of thy account."—DRYDEN.

"Jack Frost looked forth one still clear night,   And he said, 'Now I shall be out of sight; So over the valley and over the height In silence I'll take my way.'"—GOULD.

Again I faced the same task with a fresh mind and fresh hopes, all that remained with me of my former attempts being nineteen lessons.

Having detailed the two patrols and the guard on Waschout Hill as already described, I spent some twenty minutes—whilst the stores, etc., were being arranged—in walking about to choose a position to hold in the light of my nineteen lessons.

I came to the conclusion that it was not any good being near the top of a hill and yet not at the top. I would make my post on the top of Waschout Hill, where I could not be overlooked from any place within rifle-range, and where I should, I believed, have "command." I was not quite certain what "command" meant, but I knew it was important—it says so in the book; besides, in all the manoeuvres I had attended and tactical schemes I had seen, the "defence" always held a position on top of a hill or ridge. My duty was plain: Waschout Hill seemed the only place which did not contravene any of the nineteen lessons I had learnt, and up it I walked. As I stood near one of the huts, I got an excellent view of the drift and its southern approach just over the bulge of the hill, and a clear view of the river further east and west. I thought at first I would demolish the few grass and matting huts which, with some empty kerosene tins and heaps of bones and debris, formed the Kaffir kraal, but on consideration I decided to play cunning, and that this same innocent-looking Kaffir kraal would materially assist me to hide my defences. I made out my plan of operations in detail, and we had soon conveyed all our stores up to the top of the hill, and started work.

Upon the return of the patrols with their prisoners, the Dutchmen and "boys" were told off to dig for themselves and their females. The Kaffirs of the kraal we had impressed to assist at once.

My arrangements were as follows: All round the huts on the hill-top, and close to them we dug some ten short lengths of deep firing-trench, curved in plan, and each long enough to hold five men. These trenches had extremely low parapets, really only serving as rifle-rests, some of the excavated earth being heaped up behind the trenches to the height of a foot or so, the remainder being dealt with as described later. In most cases the parapets were provided with grooves to fire through at ground-level, the parapet on each side being high enough to just protect the head. As with the background the men's heads were not really visible, it was unnecessary to provide proper loopholes, which would have necessitated also the use of new sandbags, which would be rather conspicuous and troublesome to conceal. When the men using these trenches were firing, their heads would be just above the level of the ground. These firing-trenches having been got well under way, the communication trenches were started. These were to be narrow and deep, leading from one trench to the next, and also leading from each trench back to four of the huts, which were to be arranged as follows, to allow of men to fire standing up without being seen. Round the inside of the walls of these huts part of the excavated earth, of which there was ample, would be built up with sand bags, piece of anthill, stones, etc., to a height that a man can fire over, about four and a half feet, and to a thickness of some two and a half feet at the top, and loopholes, which would be quite invisible, cut through the hut sides above this parapet. There was room in each hut for three men to fire. In three of them I meant to place my best shots, to act as snipers, as they would have a more favorable position than the men in the trenches below, and the fourth was a conning tower for myself. All the tents and stores were stacked inside one of the huts out of sight.

That evening, in spite of the hardness of the work, which caused much grousing among my men, we had got the firing trenches complete, but the others were not finished—they were only half the necessary depth. The earth-walls inside the huts were also not quite completed. The Kaffirs and Dutch had deep pits, as before, in three of the huts. Ammunition and rations were distributed round the trenches the last thing before we turned in. I also had all water-bottles and every vessel that would hold water, such as empty tins, Kaffir gourds, and cooking-pots, filled and distributed in case of a long and protracted fight. Having issued orders as to the necessity for the greatest secrecy in not giving away our position should Boers turn up early next morning, I went to sleep with confidence. We had, anyhow, a very good position, and though our communications were not quite perfect, these we could soon improve if we had any time to ourselves the next morning.

Next morning broke; no enemy in sight. This was excellent, and before daylight we were hard at it, finishing the work still undone. By this time the men had fully entered into the spirit of the thing, and were quite keen on surprising Brother Boer if possible. While the digging was proceeding, the "dixies" were being boiled for the breakfasts inside four grass-screens, some of which we found lying about, so as to show nothing but some very natural smoke above the kraal. I picked out one or two of my smartest N.C.O.'s, and instructed them to walk down the hill in different directions to the river-bank and try if they could see the heads of the men in the firing trenches against the sky.

If so, the heaps of earth, tins, bones, grass-screens, etc., should be re-arranged so as to give a background to every man's head.

To review the place generally, I and my orderly walked off some half-mile to the north of the river. As we were going some distance, we doffed our helmets and wrapped ourselves in two beautiful orange and magenta striped blankets, borrowed from our Kaffir lady guests, in case any stray Boer should be lurking around, as he might be interested to see two "khakis" wandering about on the veldt. It was awkward trying to walk with our rifles hidden under our blankets, and, moreover, every two minutes we had to look around to see if the sentry at the camp had signalled any enemy in sight. This was to be done by raising a pole on the highest hut. The result of our work was splendid. We saw a Kaffir kraal on a hill, and to us "it was nothing more." There were the heaps of debris usually round a kraal, looking most natural, but no heads were visible, and no trenches. There was only one fault, and that was that a few thoughtless men began, as we looked, to spread their brown army blankets out in the sun on top of the huts and on the veldt. To the veriest new chum these square blots, like squares of brown sticking-plaster all around the kraal, would have betokened something unusual. To remedy this before it was too late I hastened back.

After we had done our breakfasts, and some three hours after dawn, the sentry in one of the huts reported a force to the north. We could do nothing but wait and hope; everything was ready, and every man knew what to do. No head was to be raised nor a rifle to be fired until I whistled from my conning-tower; then every man would pop up and empty his magazine into any of the enemy in range. If we were shelled the men in the huts could at once drop into the deep trenches and be safe. Standing in my "conning-tower," from the loopholes of which I could see the drift, I thought over the possibilities before us. With great luck perhaps the Boer scouts would pass us on either side, and so allow us to lie low for the main body. With a view to seeing exactly how far I would let the latter come before opening fire, and to marking the exact spot when it would be best to give the word, I got down into the firing-trenches facing the drift and the road south to see how matters appeared from the level of the rifles. To my intense horror, I found that from these trenches neither the drift nor the road on the near bank of the river, until it got a long way south of Waschout Hill, could be seen! The bulging convexity of the hill hid all this; it must be dead ground! It was. The very spot where I could best catch the enemy, where they must pass, was not under my fire! At most, the northern loopholes of the conning tower and one other hut alone could give fire on the drift. How I cursed my stupidity! However, it was no good. I could not now start digging fresh trenches further down the hill; it would betray our whole position at once. I determined to make the best of it, and if we were not discovered by the scouts, to open fire on the main body when they were just on the other side of the river bunched up on the bank, waiting for those in front. Here we could fire on them; but it would be at a much longer range than I had intended. It was really a stroke of luck that I had discovered this serious fault, for otherwise we might have let the bulk of the enemy cross the drift without discovering the little fact of the dead ground till too late. I reflected, also (though it was not much consolation), that I had erred in good company, for how often had I not seen a "brass-hat" ride along on horseback, and from that height fix the exact position for trenches in which the rifles would be little above the ground. These trenches, however, had not been put to the test of actual use. My error was not going to escape in the same way.

Meanwhile the enemy's scouts had advanced in much the same way as detailed before, except that after coming past Incidentamba Farm they had not halted suspiciously, but came on in small groups or clumps. They crossed the river in several places and examined the bushy banks most carefully, but finding no "khakis" there, they evidently suspected none on the open veldt beyond them, for they advanced "any way" without care. Several of the clumps joined together, and came on chatting in one body of some thirty men. Would they examine the kraal, or would they pass on? My heart beat. The little hill we were on would, unluckily, be certain to prove an attraction for them, because it was an excellent vantage ground whence to scan the horizon to the south, and to signal back to the main body to the north. The kraal was also a suitable place to off-saddle for a few minutes while the main body came up to the drift, and it meant possibly a fire, and therefore a cup of coffee. They rode up towards it laughing, chatting, and smoking, quite unsuspecting. We uttered no sound. Our Dutch and Kaffir guests uttered no sound either, for in their pits was a man with a rifle alongside them. At last they halted a moment some 250 yards away on the northeast, where the slope of the hill was more gradual and showed them all up. A few dismounted, the rest started again straight towards us. It was not magnificent, but it was war. I whistled.

*   *   *   *   *

About ten of them succeeded in galloping off, also some loose horses; five or six of them on the ground threw up their hands and came into the post. On the ground there remained a mass of kicking horses and dead or groaning men. The other parties of scouts to east and west had at once galloped back to the river, where they dismounted under cover and began to pepper us. Anyway, we had done something.

As soon as our immediate enemy were disposed of, we opened fire on the main body some 1,500 yards away, who had at once halted and opened out. To these we did a good deal of damage, causing great confusion, which was comforting to watch. The Boer in command of the main body must have gathered that the river-bed was clear, for he made a very bold move; he drove the whole of the wagons, etc., straight on as fast as possible over the odd 400 yards to the river and down the drift into the river-bed, where they were safe from our fire. Their losses must have been heavy over this short distance, for they had to abandon two of their wagons on the way to the river. This was done under cover of the fire from a large number of riflemen, who had at once galloped up to the river-bank, dismounted, and opened fire at us, and also of two guns and a pompom, which had immediately been driven a short distance back and then outwards to the east and west. It was really the best thing he could have done, and if he had only known that we could not fire on the ground to the south of the drift, he might have come straight on with a rush.

We had so far scored; but now ensued a period of stalemate. We were being fired at from the river-bank on the north, and from anthills, etc., pretty well all round, and were also under the intermittent shell-fire from the two guns. They made most excellent practice at the huts, which were soon knocked to bits, but not till they had well served their turn. Some of the new white sandbags from inside the huts were scattered out in full view of the enemy, and it was instructive to see what a splendid target they made for rifle-fire, and how often they were hit. They must have drawn a lot of fire away from the actual trenches. Until the Boers discovered that they could advance south from the drift without being under rifle-fire from our position, they were held up.

Would they discover it? As they had ridden all round us by now, well out of range, they must know all about us and our isolation.

After dark, by which time we had one man killed and two wounded, the firing died away into a continuous but desultory rifle-fire, with an occasional dropping shell from the guns. Under cover of dark, I tried to guard the drift and dead ground to the south of it, by men standing up and firing at that level, but towards midnight I was forced to withdraw them into the trenches, after several casualties, as the enemy then apparently woke up and kept up a furious rifle-fire upon us for over an hour. During this time the guns went through some mysterious evolutions. At first we got it very hot from the north, where the guns had been all along. Then suddenly a gun was opened on us away from the southwest, and we were shelled for a short time from both sides. After a little the shelling on the north ceased, and continued from the southwest only for twenty minutes. After this the guns ceased, and the rifle-fire also gradually died away.

When day dawned not a living soul was to be seen; there were the dead men, horses, and the deserted wagons. I feared a trap, but gradually came to the conclusion the Boers had retired. After a little we discovered the river-bed was deserted as well, but the Boers had not retired. They had discovered the dead ground, and under the mutually supporting fire of their guns, which had kept us to our trenches, had all crossed the drift and trekked south.

True, we were not captured, and had very few losses, and had severely mauled the enemy, but they had crossed the drift. It must have evidently been of great importance to them to go on, or they would have attempted to capture us, as they were about 500 to our 50.

I had failed in my duty.

During the next few hours we buried the dead, tended the wounded, and took some well-earned rest, and I had ample leisure to consider my failure and the causes. The lessons I derived from the fight were:

20. Beware of convex hills and dead ground. Especially take care to have some place where the enemy must come under your fire. Choose the exact position of your firing-trenches, with your eye at the level of the men who will eventually use them.

21. A hill may not, after all, though it has "command," be the best place to hold necessarily.

22. A conspicuous "bluff" trench may cause the enemy to waste much ammunition, and draw fire away from the actual defences.

In addition to these lessons, another little matter on my mind was what my colonel would say at my failure.

Lying on my back, looking up at the sky, I was trying to get a few winks of sleep myself before we started to improve our defences against a possible further attack, but it was no use, sleep evaded me.

The clear blue vault of heaven was suddenly overcast by clouds, which gradually assumed the frowning face of my colonel. "What? You mean to say, Mr. Forethought, the Boers have crossed?" But, luckily for me, before more could be said, the face began slowly to fade away like that of the Cheshire Puss in "Alice in Wonderland," leaving nothing but the awful frown across the sky. This too finally dissolved, and the whole scene changed. I had another dream.

Sixth Dream

"Sweet are the uses of adversity."

Once more was I fated to essay the task of defending Duffer's Drift. This time I had twenty-two lessons below my belt to help me out, and in the oblivion of my dream I was saved that sense of monotony which by now may possibly have overtaken you, "gentle reader."

After sending out the patrols, and placing a guard on Waschout Hill, as already described, and whilst the stores were being collected, I considered deeply what position I should take up, and walked up to the top of Waschout Hill to spy out the land. On the top I found a Kaffir kraal, which I saw would assist me much to concealment should I decide to hold this hill. This I was very inclined to do, but after a few minutes' trial of the shape of the ground, with the help of some men walking about down below, and my eyes a little above ground-level—I found that its convexity was such that, to see and fire on the drift and the approach on the south side, I should have to abandon the top of the hill, and so the friendly concealment of the Kaffir huts, and take up a position on the open hillside some way down. This was, of course, quite feasible, especially if I held a position at the top of the hill as well, near the huts on the east and southeast sides; but, as it would be impossible to really conceal ourselves on the bare hillside, it meant giving up all idea of surprising the enemy, which I wished to do. I must, therefore, find some other place which would lend itself to easy and good concealment, and also have the drift or its approaches under close rifle-fire. But where to find such a place?

As I stood deep in thought, considering this knotty problem, an idea gently wormed itself into my mind, which I at once threw out again as being absurd and out of the question. This idea was—to hold the river bed and banks on each side of the drift! To give up all idea of command, and, instead of seeking the nearest high ground, which comes as natural to the student of tactics as rushing for a tree does to a squirrel, to take the lowest ground, even though it should be all among thick cover, instead of being nicely in the open.

No, it was absolutely revolutionary, and against every canon I had ever read or heard of; it was evidently the freak of a sorely tried and worried brain. I would none of it, and I put it firmly from me. But the more I argued to myself the absurdity of it, the more this idea obtained possession of me. The more I said it was impossible, the more allurements were spread before me in its favor, until each of my conscientious objections was enmeshed and smothered in a network of specious reasons as to the advantages of the proposal.

I resisted, I struggled, but finally fell to temptation, dressed up in the plausible guise of reason. I would hold the river-bed.

The advantages I thus hoped to obtain were—

Perfect concealment and cover from sight.

Trenches and protection against both rifle and gun fire practically ready made.

Communications under good cover.

The enemy would be out in the open veldt except along the river-bank, where we, being in position first, would still have the advantage.

Plentiful water-supply at hand.

True, there were a few dead animals near the drift, and the tainted air seemed to hang heavy over the river-bed, but the carcasses could be quickly buried under the steep banks, and, after all, one could not expect every luxury.

As our clear field of fire, which in the north was only bounded by the range of our rifles, was on the south limited by Waschout Hill, a suitable position for the enemy to occupy, I decided to hold the top of it as well as the river-bed. All I could spare for this would be two N.C.O.'s and eight men, who would be able to defend the south side of the hill, the north being under our fire from the river-bank.

Having detailed this party, I gave my instructions for the work, which was soon started. In about a couple of hours the patrols returned with their prisoners, which were dealt with as before.

For the post on Waschout Hill, the scheme was that the trenches should be concealed much in the same way as described in the last dream, but great care should be taken that no one in the post should be exposed to rifle-fire from our main position in the river. I did not wish the fire of the main body to be in any degree hampered by a fear of hitting the men on Waschout Hill, especially at night. If we knew it was not possible to hit them, we could shoot freely all over the hill. This detachment was to have a double lot of water-bottles, besides every available receptacle collected in the kraal, filled with water, in anticipation of a prolonged struggle.

The general idea for the main defensive position was to hold both sides of the river, improving the existing steep banks and ravines into rifle-pits to contain from one to four men. These could, with very little work, be made to give cover from all sides. As such a large amount of the work was already done for us, we were enabled to dig many more of these pits than the exact number required for our party. Pathways leading between these were to be cut into the bank, so that we should be able to shift about from one position to another. Besides the advantage this would give us in the way of moving about, according as we wished to fire, it also meant that we should probably be able to mislead the enemy as to our numbers—which, by such shifting tactics might, for a time at least, be much exaggerated. The pits for fire to the north and south were nearly all so placed as to allow the occupants to fire at ground-level over the veldt. They were placed well among the bushes, only just sufficient scrub being cut away to allow a man to see all round, without exposing the position of his trench. On each side of the river, just by the drift, were some "spoil" heaps of earth, excavated from the road ramp. These stood some five or six feet above the general level, and were as rough as the banks in outline. These heaps were large enough to allow of a few pits being made on them, which had the extra advantage of height. In some of the pits, to give head-cover, loopholes of sandbags were made, though in most cases this was not needed, owing to the concealment of the bushes. I found it was necessary to examine personally every loophole, and correct the numerous mistakes made in their construction. Some had the new clean sandbags exposed to full view, thus serving as mere whited sepulchres to their occupants, others were equally conspicuous from their absurd cock-shy appearance, others were not bullet-proof, whilst others again would allow of shooting in one direction, or into the ground at a few yards' range, or up into the blue sky. As I corrected all these faults I thought that loopholes not made under supervision might prove rather a snare.

The result was, in the way of concealment, splendid. From these pits with our heads at ground-level we could see quite clearly out on to the veldt beyond, either from under the thicker part of the bushes or even through those which were close to our eyes. From the open, on the other hand, we were quite invisible, even from 300 yards' distance, and would have been more so had we had the whiskers of the "brethren." It was quite evident to me that these same whiskers were a wise provision of nature for this very purpose and part of her universal scheme of protective mimicry.

The numerous small dongas and rifts lent themselves readily to flanking fire, and in many places the vertical banks required no cutting in order to give ideal protection against even artillery.

In others, the sides of the crooked waterways had to be merely scooped out a little, or a shelf cut to stand upon.

In one of these deeper ravines two tents, which, being below ground-level, were quite invisible, were pitched for the women and children, and small caves cut for them in case of a bombardment. The position extended for a length of some 150 yards on each side of the drift along both banks of the river, and at its extremities, where an attack was most to be feared, pits were dug down the river-banks and across the dry river-bed. These also were concealed as well as possible. The flanks or ends were, of course, our greatest danger, for it was from here we might expect to be rushed, and not from the open veldt. I was undecided for some time as to whether to clear a "field of fire" along the river-banks or not, as I had no wish to give away our presence by any suspicious nudity of the banks at each end of our position. I finally decided, in order to prevent this, to clear the scrub for as great a range as possible from the ends of the position, everywhere below the ground-level, and also on the level ground, except for a good fringe just on the edges of the banks. This fringe I thought would be sufficient to hide the clearance to any one not very close. I now blessed the man who had left us some cutting tools. Whilst all this was being carried out, I paced out some ranges to the north and south, and these we marked by a few empty tins placed on ant-heaps, etc.

At dusk, when we had nearly all the pits finished and some of the clearance done, tents and gear were hidden, ammunition and rations distributed to all, and orders in case of an attack given out. As I could not be everywhere, I had to rely on the outlying groups of men fully understanding my aims beforehand, and acting on their "own." To prevent our chance of a close-range volley into the enemy being spoilt by some over-zealous or jumpy man opening fire at long range, I gave orders that fire was to be held as long as possible, and that no man was to fire a shot until firing had already commenced elsewhere (which sounded rather Irish), or my whistle sounded. This was unless the enemy were so close to him that further silence was useless. Firing having once started, every man was to blaze away at any enemy within range as judged by our range marks. Finally, we turned in to our pits for the night with some complacency, each eight men furnishing their own sentry.

We had about three hours next morning before any enemy were reported from Waschout Hill (the pre-arranged signal for this was the raising of a pole from one of the huts). This time was employed in perfecting our defences in various ways. We managed to clear away the scrub in the dry river-bed and banks for some 200 yards beyond our line of pits on each side, and actually attained to the refinement of an "obstacle;" for at the extremity of this clearance a sort of abatis entanglement was made with the wire from an adjacent fence which the men had discovered. During the morning I visited the post on Waschout Hill, found everything correct, and took the opportunity of showing the detachment the exact limits of our position in the river-bed, and explained what we were going to do. After about three hours' work, "Somebody in sight" was signalled, and we soon after saw from our position a cloud of dust away to the north. This force, which proved to be a commando, approached as already described in the last dream; all we could do meanwhile was to sit tight in concealment. Their scouts came on in clumps of twos and threes which extended over some mile of front, the centre of the line heading for the drift. As the scouts got closer, the natural impulse to make for the easiest crossing place was obeyed by two or three of the parties on each side of the one approaching the drift, and they inclined inwards and joined forces with it. This was evidently the largest party we could hope to surprise, and we accordingly lay for it. When about 300 yards away, the "brethren" stopped rather suspiciously. This was too much for some man on the east side, who let fly, and the air was rent by the rattle as we emptied our magazines, killing five of this special scouting party and two from other groups further out on either side. We continued to fire at the scouts as they galloped back, dropping two more, and also at the column which was about a mile away, but afforded a splendid target till it opened out.

In a very few moments our position was being shelled by three guns, but with the only result, as far as we were concerned, of having one man wounded by shell-fire, though the firing went on slowly till dark. To be accurate, I should say the river was being shelled, our position incidentally, for shells were bursting along the river for some half mile. The Boers were evidently quite at sea as regards the extent of our position and strength, and wasted many shells. We noticed much galloping of men away to the east and west, out of range, and guessed that these were parties who intended to strike the river at some distance away, and gradually work along the bed, in order probably to get into close range during the night.

We exchanged a few shots during the night along the river bed, and not much was done on either side, though of course we were on the qui vive all the time; but it was not till near one in the morning that Waschout Hill had an inning.

As I had hoped, the fact that we held the kraal had not been spotted by the enemy, and a large body of them, crawling up the south side of the hill in order to get a good fire on to us in the river, struck a snag in the shape of a close-range volley from our detachment. As the night was not very dark, in the panic following the first volley our men were able (as I learnt afterwards) to stand right up and shoot at the surprised burghers bolting down the hill. However, their panic did not last long, to judge by the sound, for after the first volley from our Lee-Metfords and the subsequent minute's independent firing, the reports of our rifles were soon mingled with the softer reports of the Mausers, and we shortly observed flashes on our side of Waschout Hill. As these could not be our men, we knew the enemy were endeavoring to surround the detachment. We knew the ranges fairly well, and though, as we could not see our sights, the shooting was rather guesswork, we soon put a stop to this manoeuvre by firing a small volley from three or four rifles at each flash on the hill-side. So the night passed without much incident.

During the dark we had taken the opportunity cunningly to place some new white sandbags (which I had found among the stores) in full view at some little distance from our actual trenches and pits. Some men had even gone further, and added a helmet here and a coat there peeping over the top. This ruse had been postponed until our position was discovered, so as not to betray our presence, but after the fighting had begun no harm was done by it. Next morning it was quite a pleasure to see the very accurate shooting made by "Brother" at these sandbags, as betokened by the little spurts of dust.

During this day the veldt to the north and south was deserted by the enemy except at out-of-range distance, but a continuous sniping fire was kept up along the river-banks on each side. The Boer guns were shifted—one to the top of Incidentamba and one to the east and west in order to enfilade the river bank—but, owing to our good cover, we escaped with two killed and three wounded. The enemy did not shell quite such a length of river this time. I confidently expected an attack along the river bank that night, and slightly strengthened my flanks, even at the risk of dangerously denuding the north bank. I was not disappointed.

Under cover of the dark, the enemy came up to within, perhaps, 600 yards on the open veldt on the north and round the edges of Waschout Hill, on the south, and kept up a furious fire, probably to distract our attention, whilst the guns shelled us for about an hour. As soon as the gun-fire ceased they tried to rush us along the river-bed east and west, but owing to the abatis and the holes in the ground, and the fact that it was not a very dark night, they were unsuccessful. However, it was touch and go, and a few of the Boers did succeed in getting into our position only to be bayoneted. Luckily the enemy did not know our strength, or rather our weakness, or they would have persisted in their attempt and succeeded; as it was, they must have lost 20 or 30 men killed and wounded.

Next morning, with so many men out of my original 40 out of action (not to include Waschout Hill, whose losses I did not know), matters seemed to be serious, and I was greatly afraid that another night would be the end of us. I was pleased to see that the detachment on Waschout Hill had still got its tail well up, for they had hoisted a red rag at the masthead. True, this was not the national flag, probably only a mere handkerchief, but it was not white. The day wore on with intermittent shelling and sniping, and we all felt that the enemy must have by now guessed our weakness, and were saving themselves for another night attack, relying upon our being tired out. We did our best to snatch a little sleep by turns during the day, and I did all I could to keep the spirits of the little force up by saying that relief could not be very far off. But it was with a gloomy desperation at best that we saw the day wear on and morning turn into afternoon.

The Boer guns had not been firing for some two hours, and the silence was just beginning to get irritating and mysterious, when the booming of guns in the distance aroused us to the highest pitch of excitement. We were saved! We could not say what guns these were—they might be British or Boer—but, any way, it proved the neighborhood of another force. All faces lighted up, for somehow the welcome sound at once drew the tired feeling out of us.

In order to prevent any chance of the fresh force missing our whereabouts, I collected a few men and at once started to fire some good old British volleys into the scrub, "Ready—present—fire," which were not to be mistaken. Shortly afterwards we heard musketry in the distance, and saw a cloud of dust to the northeast. We were relieved!

$$*\quad*\quad*\quad*\quad*$$

Our total losses were 11 killed and 15 wounded; but we had held the drift, and so enabled a victory to be won. I need not here touch upon the well-known and far-reaching results of the holding of Duffer's Drift, of the prevention thereby of Boer guns, ammunition, and reinforcements reaching one of their sorely pressed forces at a critical moment, and the ensuing victory gained by our side. It is now, of course, all public knowledge that this was the turning-point in the war, though we, the humble instruments, did not know what vital results hung upon our action.

That evening the relieving force halted at the drift, and, after burying the dead, we spent some time examining the lairs of the Boer snipers, the men collecting bits of shell and cartridge-cases as mementoes—only to be thrown away at once. We found some 25 dead and partially buried Boers, to whom we gave burial.

That night I did not trek, but lay down (in my own breeches and spotted waistcoat). As the smoke from the "prime segar," presented to me by my Colonel, was eddying in spirals over my head, these gradually changed into clouds of rosy glory, and I heard brass bands in the distance playing a familiar air: "See the Conquering Hero comes," it was they were playing.

I felt a tap on my shoulder, and heard a gentle voice say, "Arise, Sir Backsight Forethought;" but in a trice my dream of bliss was shattered—the gentle voice changed into the well-known croak of my servant. "Time to pack your kit on the wagon, sir. Corfy's been up some time now, sir." I was still in stinking old Dreamdorp.